DEDICATION

**This book is dedicated to Alice Curry.
Thank you for a solid foundation.
I miss and love you.**

GAME

Jax is an amazing basketball player.
He works with his teammates, and together
they made it to the championship GAME.

With 10 seconds left on the clock, and the score tied 35-35, Jax signals the play as the crowd begins the countdown.

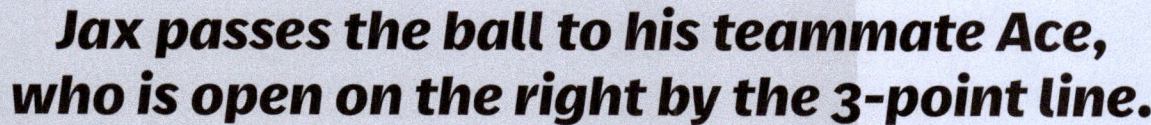

Jax passes the ball to his teammate Ace, who is open on the right by the 3-point line.

The crowd is signing and yelling,
"**SHOOT** THE BALL!"

7

Jax cuts down low under the basket and catches the pass by Ace.

The other team's defense blocked Jax's easy fade away jump shot.

Now the crowd is going wild, counting down, and roaring, "FIIIVE AND SHOOT!"

Blake, Jax's teammate, grabs the rebound and kicks it back out to Marcus at the 3-point line.

Every person in the crowd is screaming and signing, "**THREEE!**"

2

Aaron sets a screen for Marcus, who takes one dribble then passes the ball to Jax.

Jax and his team win the championship 37-35!

THE END

1

2

6

7

8

3

4

5

9

10

Game

ACKNOWLEDGMENT

The hard days are the best because that's where champions are made.

Gabby Douglas

Meet Author
Dr. Yolanda M. Carter

Dr. Yolanda M. Carter strives to implement an exciting, positive, and unique learning experience for readers of all ages. Her dedication to bringing a diverse experience to reading is inspiring to adults and children. Dr. Carter provides a pleasant spin to learning a new language. "I am not 100% fluent in sign language, however, I am working on it" says Dr. Carter. Dr. Carter is drawn to the emotions needed to engage in conversation while signing.